BRISTOL PUBLIC LIBRARIES

RESERVE

The period of loan is fourteen days and this book should be
returned on or before the date last stamped below.   A fine will
be charged for the retention of the book beyond the due date.

889 Lib   P&S

How I Make Woodcuts & Wood Engravings

by

Hans Alexander Mueller

AMERICAN ARTISTS GROUP, Inc., NEW YORK · 1945

HOW I MAKE WOOD CUTS AND WOOD ENGRAVINGS

COPYRIGHT, 1945, BY

HANS ALEXANDER MUELLER

PRINTED IN THE UNITED STATES OF AMERICA

DESIGNED BY A. A. VERSH

꒰ I love the woodcut as a form of artistic expression because it requires the simplest materials and comparative muscular strength. I love to exploit the full use of my five senses when wood, paper and color come within my grasp.

H. A. M.

Contents

HOW I MAKE WOODCUTS AND
WOOD ENGRAVINGS

The Woodcut and Wood Engraving and its place in the Graphic Arts

CHAPTER I

ᑬ TO ALMOST EVERY ARTIST there comes a time when he feels the urge to make a woodcut. The result is often exciting, although not necessarily a woodcut in the sense of manifesting a true mastery of the craft.

There is a keen, fresh pleasure in cutting into a block of wood with knife or graver to bring forth a composition of different levels, of heights and depths; and, in the ensuing printing, in rolling the black ink over the surface and pulling the first proof. The process is as unpredictable as the result. There is breathless suspense in awaiting the outcome, which always has an element of surprise. For the past few hours I have been cutting, graving, boring, gouging, scraping and scratching, and the result of my work appears suddenly before me as a whole the instant I lift the paper from the inked block. The contrast between the darkened surface of the block and the lighter shade of the natural wood which shows in the cutting is much less than the bold contrast of black ink on white paper.

The visual experience is, therefore, entirely different from that in painting or sketching, where the visible result keeps pace with the progress of the work. No wonder, then, that the first proof makes a profound impression and immediately captivates the creator's eye. Whether or not anything artistically worthwhile has been accomplished can be decided only after the first intoxication has passed.

Always there is the danger of bluffing, or of glossing over imperfections. This danger, incidentally, has subtly insinuated itself into the whole field of the graphic arts, and concerns not only the woodcut. It is most obvious in etching, where the untalented artist achieves the easiest result. Etchings are the most popular form of print in the art shops. The very name elicits from the layman a degree of respect, and gives him a mystic thrill which affects him so deeply that he has no urge to examine its source. Seldom does he have any idea of the technical process involved. All he wants of art is a thrill—perhaps the rudimentary thrill of possession. The word "etching" has a greater appeal to his romantic imagination than the more homely word "woodcut."

In the technique of etching the chief danger lies in possible accident or in deliberate trickery. In drypoint, for instance, there is the tendency to leave a lot of roughness. Later, when the ink is applied, this will widen the needle-lines three-or-four-fold. Then, in the printing of an etched plate, much ink may be applied, or the acid for etching may be permitted to bite deeply and wide. Veritable mountain ranges will appear on the paper, as though made of lava or bronze, and will be called evidences of temperament and sensuousness. Once during my student days I placed a copperplate in the acid bath, intending to let it etch for an hour, and then forgot to take it out. It spent the night there. Ruefully, nine hours later, I pulled it out, convinced that it was ruined. The result—lava, bronze, "temperament," general applause.

To all of this, copper engraving is an exception—an unique exception. This technique demands skill from artist and engraver alike. Unfortunately, in America it is comparatively little used.

In the woodcut, the temptation to bluff lies in the effectiveness of the simple black-and-white style and in the appealing freshness of the technical execution, which gives the illusion of strength and conceals inner sterility. Even a paltry drawing translated into a woodcut has a greater chance of succeeding, of getting to "look like something."

From this it follows that the clever dilettante will aways prefer one of the print-making processes to any other artistic medium. In the right hands, the woodcut affords the artist a highly concentrated means of conveying strength and integrity. Without these qualities it is a mere superficial eye-catcher.

*   *   *

Modern woodcutting and wood engraving was born when photomechanical methods of reproduction replaced the work of the older woodcutter or wood engraver. This field, which had lain fallow for a long time, was now approached by artists with caution and timidity.

Since most artists who desired to practice wood engraving as a creative art had not learned the technique of reproductive wood engraving, which is seldom taught in these days, at first they groped their way in darkness. There was a hush before the breaking of the storm, and when it came it appeared in a new form. The artist had sighted unexplored land and found revolutionary possibilities in the new woodcut as a means of expression. Instead of the graver and boxwood block which the reproductive woodcutters had used, he chose a softer wood and a knife and gave vent to his emotion in these materials when brush and pencil no longer satisfied him.

We know that the woodcut (that is, cutting with a knife in the long-grain block), was in vogue during the Expressionist (1910-1925) period, and even at the present time it is used more than any other of the graphic arts to convey the artist's more exalted moods. This applies, it seems to me, especially in Germany, and particularly to the revolutionary period at the end of the World War, at which time there was an abrupt break with almost every existing tradition. The possibilities of this new graphic medium of expression quickly made it popular among the artists. An entirely new style of print appeared. Anything was justified so long as it was expressive. Rarely did the artist hark back to the woodcut of the middle ages—the line woodcut.

Gradually woodcutting was taken up by a wider circle of artists, and soon it was introduced into the art schools. It grew more sedate and more settled. The artist began to concern himself more seriously with the fascinating crafts of cutting and engraving, casting occasional glances at the best examples of woodcuts of the reproductive period, which showed almost superhuman virtuosity. For years he tried out his knife on all kinds of woods, from the most delicate to the coarsest grained. He produced significant broadsides and portfolios in hitherto unknown formats. In every center of culture the woodcut came to be recognized as a rowdy, but by no means negligible, member of the graphic arts family.

After a while it quieted down still further. It settled into a smaller format, took on a more modest, cultured appearance; it showed its tranquil side. The versatility of the medium began to be recognized by artists. It presented itself, further, in a new guise, that of the wood engraving. And this meant that artists especially enamored of craftsmanship undertook long years of practice to master the engraving technique. Then wood engraving moved naturally into its true sphere, that of book illustration.

Nevertheless it has not yet found a perfect haven. I have the feeling that the woodcut will always be the problem child among the original printmaking processes. The technique of the woodcut is very simple, while that of the wood engraving is laborious and time-consuming, and beset with problems of style which are not inherent to the etching. I shall try to explain this.

Etching is an intaglio surface, while the woodcut is relief. The

SELF PORTRAIT OF THE AUTHOR

Engraved in Wood

indentation in the copper plate, made with a needle or acid, is designed to come out black in the proof. The indentation made with knife or graver on the wood block will be white in the proof. In printing, the copper plate is spread with ink, which is then wiped off the surface, permitting the ink to remain only in the depressions of the plate, and in the printing the ink is pressed onto the paper. The wood block, on the other hand, is inked in such a manner that only the surface receives the color, not the indentations. The lines in the copper plate correspond to black lines on white paper; in the woodblock they correspond to white chalk lines on a blackboard.

1   2

If my conception of a woodcut is such that I wish to show black lines on a white background, then I must cut or grave away all those portions of the surface which are not part of the lines. [Illus. No. 1.] If I conceive it in such a style that the result is to be white lines on a dark ground, then these lines must be cut deep into the block. [Illus. No. 2.] The preliminary consideration of what should be white and what black is as important as the style in determining the final interplay of black and white. The nature of etching does not include this double possibility.

I will not attempt to deal with lithography (planography), for I have too high a respect for this noble art, with its technical complexity and flexibility, its sensitivity and expressiveness, to dismiss it with only a few words.

The modern woodcut and wood engraving has given the artist a medium by which he can create directly on the block. The original is the carved block, and the print is made from this block. That this process allows a great number of impressions to be pulled from a single block is of secondary importance. It may be said that in the creation of a woodcut its reproductivity is not a decisive factor. This quality is of great importance, however, in the making of book illustrations. The block is the original, and no supplementary step is required in the printing of the book. Theoretically, one proof of the block is sufficient for the artist, just as the painter concludes his task with only one copy of a painting. For one, the artist will take oils and brush; for another, pencil or pastel; for a third, woodblock and knife, in accordance with the form suggested by the subject. In addition, of course, the copper plate or the lithographic stone is at his disposal.

So it follows that he will turn to the woodblock and knife or graver only when he is convinced that by this means he can best achieve the result he desires. He wishes to create an original just as much as does the painter.

The work with the knife is preceded by the most rudimentary indication of the main outlines of the design on the block. It is more than likely that the darkening of the surface will result in freeing the artist from a slavish adherence to the preliminary sketch and stimulate him to fresh expression with the knife, so that, as the interplay of light and dark develops, the design as originally planned will not be strictly followed. The preliminary sketch presents only a skeleton. It is the knife that brings out the design, in the desired black-and-white effect, which is only suggested by the rough sketch. This inevitable process again should prove that this form of graphic expression is an original medium, as opposed to the so-called woodcuts of such men as A. Menzel and G. Doré. This mistaken nomenclature (mistaken literally as well as stylistically) seems ineradicable from popular usage.

A. Menzel and G. Doré were not woodcutters. They drew their designs on the block. Then Unzelmann, the two Vogels, and others engraved the designs with the utmost accuracy.

*   *   *

It must be assumed that when an artist uses the knife creatively, the picture already exists in his mind. Whether the juxtaposition of the black and white masses is conceived in terms of light and shadow, or whether the masses produce a design entirely without reference to light and shadow, must depend on the stylistic intent. The decision is made before the manual work begins. Therefore it is unnecessary for the engraver to have a sketch in a technique approaching that of the later cutting; it would even be disturbing and hindering, because the hand guiding the knife is directed according to the stylistic purpose. Which again explains the expression "original woodcut."

Now where should the effect of black on white, or white on black, begin, and where end? Where should separation appear and where merging? For instance, I can depict a pot as a white object on a black ground, or vice versa. [Illus. Nos. 3 and 4.] Further, I can render it with both effects interchanging. [Illus. No. 5.] I can interpret it naturalistically, with lights and shadows, and in terms of space [Illus. No. 6]; or abstractly, without space, in decorative planes. [Illus. No. 7.] The selection of the black-and-white style is determined by what I want to express artistically, and that covers everything that can be explained about the nature of the woodcut. Nor will the artist himself be entirely clear when he begins to work. He gropes a good part of the way in the dark. Some time must elapse after the creation before he knows whether or not he has produced anything worthwhile.

If these matters were not inexplicable there would be no art. "Art comes from knowing; if it came from wishing, it would have to be called Wisht instead of Art."

3

4

5

6

7

Foundation of the Technique

CHAPTER II

ৡ THE UNDERLYING DESIGN of any woodcut or wood engraving is first sketched either on paper or directly onto the block with soft pencil or India ink. The second method is preferable, provided, of course, that it is unimportant whether or not the picture appears reversed in the proof.

Drawings which must not be reversed have to be mechanically transferred from paper onto the block, so that the final result will be an exact reproduction of the original. To avoid the wasteful process of tracing, an impression of the original drawing is made directly on the block. To do this the woodblock is covered with a very thin coating of any kind of soap, softened by the wet balls of the hand. The pencil drawing is then laid on the block face down and lightly fastened to it at two corners. Pressure from a hand-press or rubbing with a bone folder brings out an exact tracing on the block. [Illus. No. 8.] If the pencil used for the' drawing is not too hard, the soap will retain a great many of the graphite particles. (Use Pencil No. 3B.)

Grounding the woodblock with a white film, as was formerly done, is not advisable. The between-tones which result are irritating to the eye in the course of further work on the plate, for there will be three shades: the black of the drawing, the white of the film, and the slightly darker color of the wood which comes into play at the first cut.

Transferring a sketch by tracing is always distasteful to an artist. The freshness of his work is lost in mechanically going over the drawing and sharpening the lines with a harder pencil, and placing the carbon paper between the drawing and the block results in a copy whose lines are lifeless. The drawing which appears on the wood is perfectly correct in outline but devoid of

8

expression. The development of the work sustains a crippling blow. It is a deficiency to which beginners are especially subject.

This practical knowledge, though apparently of slight importance, was not gained overnight. It is an example of the close interdependence of a very simple technical process and a highly emotional and spiritual experience. It is in dealing with just such details that a teacher should find a field of useful activity.

After the transfer of the sketch onto the block, the composition is strengthened with black India ink, using pen or brush. Then the surface of the block is darkened with a dilution of India ink, printer's ink or graphite powder, to such a degree that, while the drawing remains visible, the deepest possible tone is obtained, in order to get the contrast between the darkened surface and the natural color of the wood which appears in cutting.

Knife, gouge and graver must be well sharpened—a skill which must also be acquired. [Illus. No. 9 shows the sharpening of a graver.] Most beginners ruin their tools, and it is often hard to determine whether an unsuccessful piece of work is due to lack of control or to a dull knife—to the artist or to the tool.

9

The artist must sit so that the light comes from the left front, or, in the case of a left-handed person, from the right front. Eyes must be shaded against the source of light; the block should be about ten inches away from the eyes; both elbows should be outspread on the table, giving the effect of a brooding swan. All remains of previous work must be cleared away.

And now the artist can begin to cut or to engrave—where and how is his concern, and each one does it differently. But now he must not be disturbed.

When he feels that his work is ready for printing, he washes off the block, first with a rag lightly moistened with benzine (not turpentine), and then with one dampened in water, to get rid of the traces of India ink. Wood is porous and tends to absorb water and become soft, which is not good for the printing.

In a few minutes the block will be dry. It is then carefully brushed in all directions, but not, of course, with a steel brush. Then the artist takes printer's ink from a can or tube, spreads a wide strip of it with a spatula on a smooth stone or glass plate, rolls out the color evenly with a printing roller into a rectangular

10

field [Illus. No. 10]. The substance of a roller or brayer is a composition of glue and jelly (not rubber). Rollers do not like sun rays and heat. Then transfer the ink to the block with the roller, being careful not to press too hard. The color spreads most evenly and quickly if it is applied to the block with criss-cross strokes of the roller, lifted at the end of each stroke and set down anew. It is useless to move the roller back and forth three or four times over the same track.

Then the paper is placed on the block and pressure is applied, either with a regular handpress or an embossing press, or, when neither is available, by rubbing with a bone folder, in which case one must be careful to avoid slipping off the edge of a line or surface. The folding bone likewise is used when the artist wishes to get variations in impression from one and the same plate— that is, where tonal gradations are not cut in the block, but are attained by more or less pressure of the hand. This gives the effect of painting. This method must be used sparingly and for highly special effects, and should be avoided altogether by beginners.

A good proof depends on three things: the amount of ink, the strength of the impression, and the structure of the paper.

The Woodcut-Long Grain

CHAPTER III

☙ THE WOODCUT IS CUT WITH A KNIFE in a block of wood with a grain running parallel to the printing surface. Such a block cannot be engraved, for the graver is not able to cut clean across the grain, but will merely tear up the fibres of the wood without removing them.

Many kinds of wood are suitable, but the most satisfactory are, in the order given, pear, plum, maple, beech, poplar, cherry and birch. Pine and fir can be used only in the execution of a greatly simplified black-and-white style, where the impression of the coarse and irregular grain of the wood is not only unavoidable but actually desirable. The very flaws and knots can heighten the bold effect of the picture. The charm of these natural materials, however, can only be brought out by supreme performance. Only a master can avoid the descent to the cheapest effects.

The woodcut is the newest medium among the original graphic arts. In it the modern artist finds the means of stylistic experimentation—a means wherewith to express with strength and precision exactly what he has in mind, and give his pictures literary content without erring in taste. But the reverse must also be kept in mind—that the very ruggedness of the medium may lead to a mere accumulation of bombastic effects.

The woodcut, technically the most primitive and most robust of all the manual processes, requiring the greatest strength of arm and hand, and richest in stylistic problems, exerts an irresistible attraction on those artists who wish to avoid being facile and equally to avoid repeating themselves *ad nauseam* or making a mere formula of their work; who delight to produce with difficulty; who want to express themselves when and how their talent demands, even in dark and sinister moods, and whose artistic character is based on the joy of story-telling and the love of working with their hands.

If, in deciding upon the artistic medium to be used, there is a choice between charcoal drawing and woodcutting—the first of which is quickly produced with slight manual effort, while the second requires strenuous hand work and a considerable expenditure of time—then there is a factor underlying the decision which definitely challenges thought. The artist makes a real choice only in those instances when it is not a matter of indifference to him which medium he uses. He is like a composer who must decide whether his musical concept demands a flute or a viola to give the proper color and character.

* * *

The natural language of the woodcut is black-and-white surfaces almost without between-tones. To express this language the actual hand work is the important thing. Inserting the knife to effect a sharp separation between two planes is certainly, so far as touch is concerned, a stronger, more expressive manner of working than evolving a black-and-white design on a sheet of paper with pen and ink, for the knife, as it divides, introduces a third dimension, depth. The visual effect of the two techniques may be about the same. But the way of the knife in the wood is much more time-consuming and arduous. If the final result is not stronger, more expressive, stylistically more significant, then the detour has been a useless expenditure of time and of energy.

It follows that this difficult path will be preferred by the artist who not only loves the stubborn, intractable nature of the woodcut, but who seeks it out in order to achieve a deliberate effect; who knows the deep inner excitement of holding in his hands the still unmutilated block and making that first cut which determines all that follows; who is aware of a deep spiritual significance when the creative mood, combined with the expression of

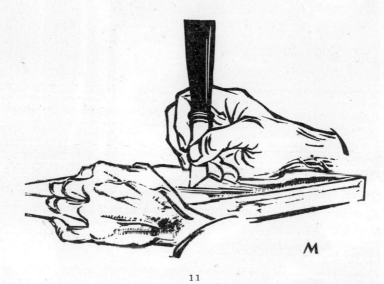

11

the strength of his arm and hand, gradually intensifies into a delirium of concentration; who, as he cuts through the grain, sees in a flash before him the very tree whose wood has now become the medium for the realization of his dream.

I should now like to reveal some of the intimacies of creation which only the artist can know. I shall touch upon them now and again in what follows, and I can only hope to succeed in handling these delicate matters without false sentiment.

*   *   *

The contrast of black and white cannot be brought out more sharply than in the long-grain woodcut. A similar effect in wood engraving would be attempted only in very small format (e.g., Masereel's *Book of Hours*). Technically the woodcut is not very well suited to small formats; the only limitation that can be set

12

to its largeness is that the whole must be taken in at a glance. [Illus. No. 12.] In woodcutting the artist strives for simplification of form and for the reduction of all tone values to two denominators, black and white. The production of between tones, easily accomplished in charcoal drawing, is certainly not forbidden, nor is it in any way detrimental to the style. But it requires a skill in handling the knife which must not be underestimated, and a knowledge of what is of real value in the final proof.

13

No other artistic process is so directly dependent on the nature of the technique as the woodcut. The straight edge of the knife has an almost malicious tendency to persist in the direction of its insertion. Only after long practice can one succeed in cutting curves. And cutting with the grain of the wood has a different feel than cutting across it or diagonally to it.

The cutting of closely parallel lines with the knife which together will give the half-tone effects [Illus. No. 13] is one of the most irksome tasks that an artist can set himself. A similar effect can be obtained more quickly and with less effort by using the gouge, but the result will not exhibit the strength of style attained by cutting with the knife.

I need not dwell on linoleum cutting as practice for wood-cutting. The simplicity and effortlessness of its technique places it within the reach of any beginner or dilettante.

Linoleum can be bought in any department store cutting off from the roll in large quantity or in art material stores mounted on a woodblock (type high). In the second case I advise to buy plates which are not white covered. The surface of the linoleum plate should have the same color as the cut. The white skin makes it easier indeed to recognize the pencil or ink drawing, but more confusing for your eye when you start cutting, because of three different shades: black drawing, white skin and color of the linoleum. Linoleum needs a little less pressure than wood.

Strangely enough, in the very nature of the woodcut lies the ability to demonstrate the connection between a technically primitive material and the abstraction of meaning achieved by it. Or should this ability portend just the opposite? It is the same inexplicable phenomenon that in music allows wood, gut and hair (the acoustical equipment of a stringed instrument) to interpret a Bach fugue, the highest form of spiritual abstraction. The most erudite explanation would still leave me far from satisfied.

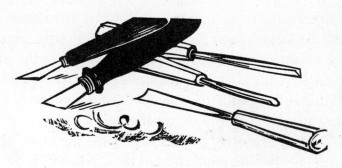

14

A few technical instructions now:

Tools: knives and gouges. [Illus. No. 14.] These are used on all long-grain blocks and linoleum.

Whetstone. To sharpen the knife, two drops of machine oil on the stone. Also, water or spittle.

In cutting, insert the knife so that the surface or line to be outlined by the cut widens slightly at the base, somewhat in the form of a stone or concrete dam. Here is a cross-section of a block, somewhat enlarged. [Illus. No. 15.] Cut deep enough. This makes it easier, later on, to rout out the areas that are not to print, as

15

the wood near the edge of the cut tends to break off of itself. This will avoid the danger of the knife hitting under the dam shaped foot of the line or surface and injuring it or even breaking it away altogether. To rout out larger areas it is better to use a gouge.

During the cutting, the block lies flat on a steady table, not on a leather sandbag like the engraving block. Particular people like to place a thick, even piece of cloth between the block and the table. It is obvious that the very slight rocking and yielding of this foundation pad will give a pleasant elasticity to the hand guiding the knife, and yet the block will not wobble.

In wood-engraving, as was just noted, the cross-grain block lies on the leather sandbag and is turned so that the plane can be worked on from all directions. The long-grain block for wood-cutting remains flat on the table. But since it, too, must be turned during the work, there is still to be invented and manufactured a vise in which the block will be firmly held so that the knife can be applied from various angles. This vise will have to rest in the middle of a round or square board about two armlengths in diameter, the turning-screw affixed with considerable tenacity. But so many artists have invented and constructed gadgets, and, for all that, their pictures don't seem to turn out any better.

WOODCUTS — LONG GRAIN

from THE CONRAD ARGOSY
by *Joseph Conrad*

from THE CONRAD ARGOSY
by Joseph Conrad

from THE CONRAD ARGOSY by Joseph Conrad

· 26 ·

from THE CONRAD ARGOSY *by Joseph Conrad*

from THE CONRAD ARGOSY
by Joseph Conrad

from THE CONRAD ARGOSY
by *Joseph Conrad*

from SON OF THE DANUBE
by Boris Petroff

from SON OF THE DANUBE
by Boris Petroff

WAR

The Wood Engraving · End Grain

CHAPTER IV

&⁓ TO EMPHASIZE THE FUNDAMENTAL DIFFERENCE in character between the woodcut and the wood engraving, I might say that, aside from the completely different technique, the engraving is the more cultured member of the pair. In saying this, I do not attempt to express a judgment of artistic values.

Engraving affords a wider range than cutting. It does not, however, give the stubborn, rebellious artist either the spiritual or technical means for making a lot of noise. Nor does it run around with hair on its chest and hobnailed boots on its feet; it is no table-thumping orator, loudly preaching a new world-philosophy; it does not have a rugged countenance or offensive manners. Perhaps it does not dig so deep, perhaps it handles problems of style more cautiously; it is more adaptable; does not demand attention at all costs; is less unkempt. Altogether, it is less of a roughneck than its brother, the woodcut.

If occasionally it does put on an act, it is on a smaller stage and before a smaller audience. Its repertory is suited to the Little Theatre, not to the Metropolitan Opera House.

* * *

The best wood used for engraving is boxwood. It is the hardest and finest-grained of all woods. There are several varieties, listed here in the order of preference: American, African, and Turkish boxwood, also maple. An ancestral boxwood tree-trunk is only as thick as that of a twelve-year-old birch. The rings of boxwood lie so close together that they are almost indistinguishable. In structure and consistency the wood resembles ivory.

In preparing an engraving block, the boxwood log is sliced across the grain and the slices stored for a number of years in a dry place. They are then sawed into small pieces and the best of

16

them glued together into rectangular plates and polished down on both sides until they are exactly type high. The engraving surface is evened off with a special scraper, rubbed down with very fine emery paper, and finally thinly coated with shellac. The block thus prepared for engraving no longer resembles wood, but rather some plastic composition. The grain of the wood runs at right angles to the printing surface, not parallel to it, as in the woodcut block. The structure of the wood is of no importance in the engraving, but the cabinet maker who prepares the blocks must leave no noticeable unevenness or seams of glue. If a seam splits or the block warps, then the wood was not sufficiently dried. After engraving also, the blocks must be kept in a cool, dry place, and must stand, not lie flat.

*   *   *

The engraving tool is the burin, of which there are hundreds of varieties, from the most pointed to the broadest. [Illus. No. 16.] It is made of very hard steel. About a third of the hemispherical handle is cut away on the under side in order to prevent its catching when the burin is held low over the block. [Illus. No.

17

17.] The tool is held in the hand so that the handle rests against the outer part of the palm at the base of the little finger. The thumb, extended towards the point of the burin, rests on the block as a support and pivot. The four fingers are drawn back and curved, lying close together on the upper edge of the burin (seen from below the tips should look like peas in a pod) and pressing the tool against the ball of the thumb. The fingers must not clasp the burin; they must be kept away from the lower edge for the same reason that the handle is cut away. There should be a hollow space between the handle and the palm of the hand.

Moving the burin forward is most difficult for the beginner. It is done by the combined strength of finger and hand muscles, not by the strength of the arm. A sort of kneading motion takes place, a restrained unfolding of strength in a forward direction which can be stopped at any moment. This drives the burin through the wood in a long, uninterrupted movement, and allows it to dip more or less deeply into the wood without breaking the rhythm or getting stuck. The motion is correct when it can be performed in the air over the block as easily as in the wood itself, and without noticeable difference. The palm of the hand vaulted over the burin and the curved back-drawn fingers create an inexhaustible reservoir of strength which has the power to bring the forward-driving force to a dead stop at will. The result is that it is most unusual to overrun the intended end of a line and damage the block—unusual, at least, in one who has mastered the engraving technique.

It seems strange to the beginner that he cannot simply take the burin in his fist, for he believes that he should be able to hold it most securely in that way. It is an anatomical fact, however, that making a fist cramps the hand and arm muscles, while, as stated above, the freedom of the hand muscles is the supreme essential needed for controlling the graver.

Anyone who has learned to play the violin knows what difficulty he had at first in holding the bow. He, too, thought, in his all-knowing ignorance, that he could take hold of the bow as though it were a stick to beat with. The realization that it must be held in the fingertips alone, came only when he found that the hand must work independently of the wrist.

When the engraver has become accustomed to the independent action of hand and wrist, the extent to which the strength of his arm may come into play will be determined automatically.

The aforementioned kneading motion of the hand pushes the burin forward onto the soft ball of the thumb. At the completion of the motion, the fingers draw the burin back again, but the thumb remains forward as a guide for the tool. The left hand presses the block against the burin and, in the cutting of curves, turns it on the axis of the right thumb, which rests on the block. The turning is facilitated by the round leather sandbag on which the block rests. Beginners must be warned to place the fingers of the left hand so that, if the burin happens to slip, it will go be-

18

tween them. Burin cuts are not dangerous, but can be quite deep. Anyhow, every engraver must get an occasional cut; it goes with the calling.

The beginner will do well to practise with the burin on a small piece of boxwood, making simple, abstract designs. He should try to engrave fifteen or twenty lines close together without having them run into one another. This exercise should be done with burins of different sizes, and with varying distances between the lines. One should not expect to make a pretty picture right away.

In fact, it makes the technical exercises easier not to think of pictures at all.

From straight lines the student advances to curves, then to circles and zigzags. Then he practises engraving a few pen-strokes which he has drawn on the block himself. First he outlines the pen lines on both sides with a fine-pointed burin; then, with graduated burins, gradually levels off the area around the lines to a depth that will not print. [Illus. Nos. 18-22.] To make this easier, he uses a small flat sliver of wood, about 1/16" thick,

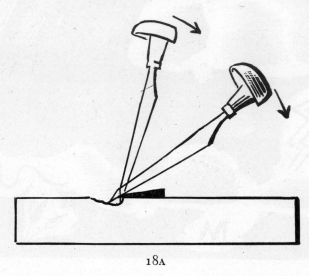

18A

tapered to a knife edge, like a small school ruler, to use as a fulcrum upon which to rock the burin and prevent slipping (See Illus. 18a.)

Another exercise for the beginner: Without any preliminary drawing, and using a broad graver, outline an irregular area on the darkened surface of the block. Then rout out the wood for about one-quarter of an inch around this area and, taking a graver which has a very sharp point but which widens rapidly, break up the outlined area into a series of lines which, beginning at the center and working toward the edges, will make a transition from black to white and leave the original outline no longer noticeable. As one works out from the center, the lines which are to appear white are gradually widened by the ever deeper incision of the burin, which is equivalent to narrowing the black lines to a hair's breadth. The fineness of the wood permits the most delicate black lines. The first proof will show whether or not the transition from

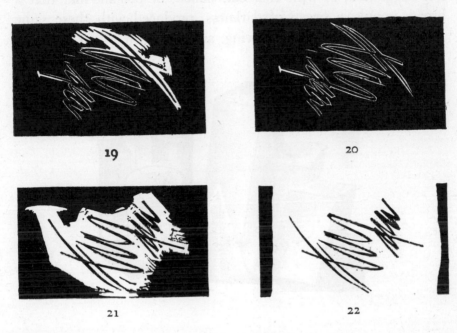

19
20
21
22

dark to light has been made successfully; if not, the individual lines must be worked over again.

Next the beginner may attempt a small design consisting of such primary forms as cubes, cylinders and prisms [Illus. No. 23], whose values may be brought out either in a chiaroscuro effect or by a changing of tonal areas without consideration of space.

After he has made several engravings of simple objects, the student may begin on landscapes or figures. He still has little or no idea how difficult it is to produce, in engraving technique, even the smallest of his earlier pen or crayon drawings, and an experienced teacher would advise him to choose an even smaller format. From his preliminary studies he has an inkling of how slow a process it is to organize an area into black and white. He has noticed that a mistake in engraving can only rarely be corrected—that there is nothing in wood engraving equivalent to the eraser. He has found that it is impossible to give a very light, free suggestion, as with charcoal, pencil, or pen-and-ink; that a broad, impulsive sweep of darkness, produced with these same media, is the privilege of drawing, and that in it, when the com-

23

position demands, as much as one-third of the space can be filled in two seconds, but that this same effect can be achieved in engraving only after cool consideration and the tedious stringing together of hundreds of engraved lines. So it is assumed that the engraver has the whole layout of the available space so clearly in mind that at the first cut he knows exactly what is to follow, although it will take four or five hours before the work is completed.

It takes several years before the engraver's imagination is so developed that he can take full advantage of all the possible variations, such as the relationship of the line groups to one another, the breaking up of the surface into dots or longer or shorter wedge-shaped strokes—the rocking of the burin vertically or horizontally.

In hacking and sawing up the surface of the block, and in effecting the crisscrossing of those white, so-called negative, effects which are the essence of the black-and-white style of the engraving, it is uncannily easy to reach a point where the surface of the block breaks down of itself, with resulting technical and pictorial emptiness. Where too much white has been introduced, black is necessarily lacking and can never be replaced. In etching there is always the possibility of repairing accidental injuries to the plate by rubbing down or hammering out from behind.

The style of the engraving, insofar as it can be put into words at all, depends on the merging of the black (positive) effects into the white (negative), and of the white effects into the black.

*　　*　　*

The wood engraving begins where the woodcut, by its very nature, must leave off—with tonal gradations.

If the woodcut, because of its material and tools, offers all the prerequisites for a style of black-and-white areas and bold contours, so the wood engraving is in its element when it employs the countless variety of effects afforded by the hard wood of the box and the rich choice of implements.

The engraving should accomplish just those things which the woodcut, because of its style, must leave undone, and vice versa. The wood used in engraving can produce the finest tonal variations, composed of innumerable little lines which the naked eye distinguishes separately only when attention is drawn to them. I have often heard the astonished exclamation: "Why, that looks like a copper or steel engraving!" And, indeed, the wood engravings of the bygone craftsmen, which were the daily fare of the illustrated papers from 1840-1890, are often much finer than copper or steel engravings.

It is quite comprehensible that some, if not many, modern artists have yielded to the matchless charm of this engraving technique, for the field has been left entirely to them. Considered as an original graphic medium, wood engraving is still quite isolated, being either completely unknown to the layman or confused by him with other techniques. Its prints are not yet given their full due of appreciation among the related arts: etching, lithography, woodcuts and copper engravings. But all of this does not keep the resolute artist from devoting all his strength and love to the craft.

The technique of tonal engraving has on its program one more

24

item for epicures, the engraving made with the so-called multiple liner. [Illus. No. 24.] This tool has the same form and function as an ordinary one-track burin, but instead of one point it has ten or twelve at the same level, and it places at the disposal of the engraver a wealth of gradations to satisfy the most demanding. But as with all such refinements—star-performances, overbreeding —the margin is very narrow; it is easy to fall into very poor stuff indeed. Technical bravura alone is nothing—it gives only a slight superficial titillation. A second glance reveals the underlying emptiness. And it is the responsibility of each artist to decide just how far to go.

But apart from this danger, the use of this consciously prepared tool gives a new form of expression to the graphic arts: a wood cut rooted entirely in a technical tradition, free from any echo of the other forms so richly at the disposal of the creative artist.

With the use of this multiple liner, engraving becomes almost superfluous. It is more like painting with a metal brush a few tenths of a millimeter into the hard polished surface of the boxwood block. The greater the pressure (that is, the deeper this sharp "brush-graver" goes into the wood), the lighter the line will appear in the print. During the work, the eye is concentrated on the direction of the tool, not on the trail it leaves behind it, which can only be seen in detail through a magnifying glass. The hand must feel its way, allowing the graver to cut more or less into the wood; and only that hand dare attempt it which, through long experience with wood, can depend on its own accuracy.

It is not necessary to use a magnifying glass; for the time being it is enough for the eye to take in the total impression of the marks left by the multiple liner. The organization of the area into groups of varying tonal values has been determined by the choice of the graver. But the darkening of the surface is still a prerequisite. Without it, not only would there be a great strain on the eyes, but it would be impossible to see where the wood had been engraved and where not. The effect would be the same as if someone were to write with white chalk on a white wall.

Every style-conscious artist will soon discover that only with the greatest caution can the multiple liner be used in combination with ordinary burins in one and the same engraving. Its accurate parallels seem painfully stiff and lifeless in contrast to the more flexible lines drawn with the one-track graver.

A mixture of these two techniques will generally cause some feeling of displeasure to the initiated observer. But there are a few cases where the multiple-line technique can be deliberately introduced into, and harmonized with, the single-track technique; namely, when the beginning and end of each line in the multiple liner group is taken up and continued, line for line, with the burin, and led from its mechanical sterility back to the easy flexibility of the other lines. Of course, the skillful and sensitive artist can override all such warnings and still be justified in the light of his particular artistic purpose (e.g., Lynd Ward). There is no greater delight and satisfaction to be found than in successfully overthrowing established doctrines and producing something on one's own account.

Used alone, and with rich technical imagination, the multiple liner, with all the subtlety of its gradations, can produce such an enchantment of tone-painting that the dangers of the technique become negligible, and he who sees a print made in this manner can no longer tell how it was made.

It was invented by a commercial woodcutter and used for a generation in a strictly subordinate role. It attained an independent position when the whole technique of wood engraving was taken over by the original reproductive processes. In the last twenty years it has particularly proved itself. It is found most often in French book illustration. The field of its usefulness has been even more enlarged with the latest development, the colored wood engraving, which, again, must not be confused with the colored woodcut.

from DR. JEKYLL AND MR. HYDE
by Robert Louis Stevenson

from DR. JEKYLL AND MR. HYDE
by Robert Louis Stevenson

Illustration for
"THE SHAKESPEAREAN TITLE PAGE MYSTERY"
Dolphin Magazine

from BOOK OF NEW YORK WOODCUTS

from BOOK OF NEW YORK WOODCUTS

from TREASURE ISLAND
by Robert Louis Stevenson

from TREASURE ISLAND
by Robert Louis Stevenson

ABRAHAM LINCOLN

THOMAS JEFFERSON

Illustrations from DON QUIXOTE
by Miquel de Cervantes Saavedra

MASARYK

The Colored Woodcut & Wood Engraving

CHAPTER V

֍ IN WORK WITH COLOR the same principle holds true for both the woodcut and the wood engraving: as many blocks as there are colors.

The colored woodcut attains its full stature in the work of the Japanese. There is nothing comparable to it in style or technique. Far as the European excels in the mastery of the black-and-white woodcut, just so far does he lag behind in the use of the colored woodcut. There are a few exceptions to this. Among them I should like to mention the work of Richard Floethe and Charles Smith, who have caught the true spirit of the colored woodcut: the equal importance of all the blocks which make up a color print. The print made with several plates, but in which a key-plate, in black, predominates I do not consider to be a colored woodcut, for the colors might just as well be added with a brush, or the key-plate allowed to stand alone. Not the number of plates, but their real necessity, is the determining factor in the colored style, and that is the only thing that counts.

The charm of a four-voice composition lies in the way each voice adds its separate color to the whole. The harmonious accompaniment of three voices to one leading voice is not, strictly speaking, a four-voice composition.

With but few exceptions, then, the colored woodcut in Europe has produced a large but somewhat feeble progeny—insignificant in style, more or less crude in color. The best of them are still inferior to the Japanese. So the colored woodcut as a whole is not comparable in importance to the black-and-white.

The colored woodcut and engraving demand great clarity in the arrangement of colors, for the bringing together of a number of colors into a complete picture is a slow sequence in contrast with painting in oil or water color. What the composite proof shows to be lacking in any one plate it is then too late to correct. In painting, the artist can jump from one color to another in a comparatively short time, which is indispensable as groundwork for composition in color, but this is not possible in woodcutting or engraving. Of course, the different colors can be tried out alongside of one another on the inking stone, but the color values of three or four plates printed on top of each other will only be seen in the final result. If this is not as desired, all the plates must be printed over again. Obviously, a woodcutter who can do this must also be a painter.

In modern colored woodcuts either water color or oil paint (printer's ink) is used. Water color is opaque, oil is transparent; water color is more fluid than oil.

If the pigment of water color is too strong, it can be thinned with water or glycerine. If the pigment of oil is too strong, it can be thinned with transparent (not opaque) white. Also, in both cases, it is possible to obtain a light shade by inking the stone with correspondingly less color.

Oil color can be made opaque by mixing opaque white with each color used. But here we are dealing with special cases.

Knowing the chief characteristics of water and oil color, as described above, the woodcutter can now determine on the color style of his picture.

When water color is used the color structure will be produced chiefly by the placing of colors next to one another. Because of the opacity of the colors, obviously if they were superimposed upon one another, the last printed would predominate. When oils are used, the structure is produced by the overlapping of the blocks. A wealth of color may be obtained in this way because of the gradations within the overlapping plates.

These basic differences in the use of water color and oil do not, of course, preclude certain modifications. Changing the consistency of either will affect the number and distribution of the plates; it is possible to make a water-color woodcut composed of several superimposed blocks and very much thinned color, or an oil color woodcut with colors printed alongside each other and the demarcations heightened by an admixture of opaque white.

Both kinds of color may be had commercially in tubes or cans. Our color chemists are experimenting with a water color for relief printing which will have the advantages, heretofore monopolized by oil, of being less fluid and more transparent. This will mean that water color can be used for colored wood engravings, too, without fear that the finest line groups will become choked with the color.

The thicker the color, the less is required. The superimposing of colors rests on this hypothesis.

Every technical variation is justified insofar as it contributes something of its own. The same holds true of style. The colored wood engraving, as opposed to the colored woodcut, shows an enrichment of the tonal variations within each individual plate. Therein lies its peculiar charm. What is gained in the way of color nuances when these already shaded plates are superimposed upon one another is not hard to imagine. But this wealth of color tone must be produced with a smaller number of blocks than the woodcut requires. A colored wood engraving in four or five plates is so artistically inclusive that the addition of another plate may

25

tend to weaken the color effect, dulling it to the eye because of
the very oversaturation of color particles.

The colored wood engraving is an entirely new phenomenon
among the original graphic arts. From the point of view of tech-

nique only, perhaps the work of a little known artist of the reproductive school, Krueger, might be considered as the product of a
forerunner. Around the turn of the century Krueger was occupied
in reproducing in color the great oil paintings of the sixteenth

25A

and seventeenth century. He was an artist of our generation with
an unequalled love of craftsmanship. His work represents the
dividing line between sedulous reproduction and artistic creation.
A unique case, so far as I know. I assume that this artist, unrecog-

25B

nized during his lifetime, has received his due of appreciation somewhere in the history of art.

In our times the colored wood engraving appears almost entirely in book illustration, and there it has found its proper sphere.

Among the few of our book illustrators who have worked exhaustively in this field, the name of the Frenchman Fernand Siméon must be prominently mentioned. The colored wood-engraved illustrations of this distinguished artist represent, in my opinion, the height of the enchantment that can be evoked by this medium. Siméon's colored prints (see "Jean des Figues" and "Chèvre d'or") stem directly from painting. They possess the greatest charm that a print can have, combining the highest degree of artistry with a fresh technique, free from routine, almost clumsy. How different they are from the work of some of our well-known contemporaries whose technical virtuosity and ossification of style through eternal repetition lead finally to a condition of spiritual devastation.

The novelty of the colored wood engraving lies in its style as well as in its technique. Here the use of the multiple liner is most important. I have already mentioned that each individual plate in a four- or five-color engraving can show within itself a greater or less degree of tonal variation, depending for its position and the direction of its lines on the desired tonal color of the composite print.

Since the style of the colored wood engraving is polyphonic and is achieved by all the single plates playing each its part, the engraver, when he considers the color sketch which forms the basis for his engraving, faces the ticklish problem of deciding which plate should come first. Experience will teach him to choose a color which appears most frequently in the picture, and which will be of medium, or light tone value—never dark. The darkest color he will keep for the last, using it to put the final accent on the picture. This procedure is exactly the opposite of that used in the earlier woodcut or engraving, which began with a key-plate and followed on with one or two plates of a purely supplementary color character.

After the earlier colors have been printed the artist will see where an accent is needed to round out the color harmony. The essence of accent lies in its sparing use. If he began with the darkest color he would always be tempted to employ too much of it because of the emptiness of the picture at that stage. It is a wearisome mental process, in engraving this darkest plate as the first, to retain constantly in the mind's eye the total color-composition; the danger is great that this darkest plate will include too much, and perhaps even become a key- or outline-plate. This would upset the stylistic conception. On the other hand if, after the first composite proof, one of the individual plates appears to contain too much, this can easily be corrected without infringing upon the character of the color style.

The multiple liner, with its wide range of tone values, is the implement which, with the least effort, produces the desired artistic effect in each individual plate as well as in the harmony of the whole. And, confidentially, a successful work of art is produced not so much through the virtuosity and capacity for the work of the artist as the uninitiated seem to think, but rather through the logical cooperation of certain determining factors which underlie the solution of any artistic problem. Even after years of experience the artist is taken by surprise by almost every work successfully completed in a new technique of which he had not dreamed before. This surprise always gives him deep if brief gratification, and remains the finest reward for a completed job.

A few further comments are necessary on the technical procedure in making colored wood engravings.

The colored wood engraving differs from the one-color engraving in that it is practically essential to have a preliminary color sketch. This sketch will show the direction of the color limitations. It is not the original; it is merely a visible guide for the mental concept of the finished engraving. The original is present in the mind of the artist, and first takes visible form as the finished print.

I do not think it will harm to repeat this again. The fact that we artists are still often asked "Did you cut the block yourself, too?" shows how little understanding there is of the true nature of the original graphic processes.

After the first block has been engraved it is inked with the allotted color and printed. Then at inconspicuous points, and as far apart as possible, little holes are made in the wood with the finest needle available. These are the so-called register points. The remaining colors, not printed in the first proof should be sketched in with colored pencils or crayons so that the complete effect is before you. In this way the artist can see whether there is too much or too little in the first plate, as well as judge of its color value. Next he makes an impression of this first plate, in black, on each of the successive plates, and immediately drills the register holes in the wood. This assures the register of all plates in the composite. He engraves the second plate after sketching in, in black ink, what this plate is to contain; then takes an impression of the first and second plates together, and again fills in, in colored pencil, the colors still to come. All the plates follow along in this manner. The process of making combined proofs of all the colors until the final proof is in hand is most complicated and delicate, and often takes longer than the engraving of the plates. The knowledge that two colors of the same tone value when superimposed produce not only a third color but also a distinctly darker shade determines the selection, mixing and quantity of the colors.

The color tone of one plate can ruin the harmony of all the others. If at the end of the process it appears that one of the earlier printed colors is at fault, the whole job goes into the waste-paper basket and the printing starts again from scratch. In most cases, each plate requires a little working over with the graver. In each plate there is apt to be a little too much—far better than too little. When at last a final proof is ready, the pulling of the edition

26

proofs can begin, for the artist no doubt will want to have a certain number of copies. Now he can begin with any plate whose color has been determined, and print the desired number. Each color must dry for a day or two before the next can be added. If the previous color is not dry, the succeeding one will not be completely absorbed. The paper takes its proper place on each successive plate because the register points are marked both on the

26A

paper and on the blocks. An imperfect print is the result of pure carelessness. To use other kinds of register depends on the difference of printing presses. I prefer the above mentioned method because of its exactness and simplicity. It is advisable during the printing to lay aside a couple of proofs of each color separately, in case reprints should be wanted at a later date. In making colored wood engravings I use only oil colors (printer's ink).

26B

As with the one-color wood engraving, there are definite limits to the size of multi-colored wood engravings. All the various gravers, as well as every movement and thrust of the hand that guides them, seem to show an instinctive surrender to surface restrictions. The command of space is limited to about the area of half a medium-sized book page. Beyond that size the woodcut in one or more colors is preferable. The tonal variations within each plate in the engraving technique might easily become tedious and boring in a large format. Wherever art begins to take visible or audible form, such limitations of style appear. It is in the stimulating of one's ability to recognize these limitations, and to fulfill oneself completely within them, that the fascination lies.

In choosing wood engraving one chooses the most roundabout way to produce a small colored picture. If the result is not something peculiarly individual, the effort is hardly worthwhile. I think I have made clear that an exceptional expenditure of effort is required for the attainment of this goal. I myself have been working on this difficult project for almost 20 years. Neither before nor during this time have I seen another woodcutter take it up, and this fact has spurred on my original love for this form of graphic art to a sort of obsession, which grows greater from job to job. Perhaps on the whole it might be called crazy, for no similar examples have appeared along the way to afford help, cheer, inspiration, or controls. Aside from the illustrative work of the Frenchman, Fernand Siméon, whom I have already mentioned, I am familiar with modern colored wood engravings only in the works of the Americans, R. Ruzicka and Th. Nason, and they cannot be classified unqualifiedly as such, since the black plate predominates both stylistically and visually in their work. So I feel at once isolated and encouraged. Perhaps the trail that I am blazing will cross that of another still unknown to me.

*   *   *

The two-tone engraving or woodcut closely parallels the multicolored. Needless to say I do not mean the cut or engraving of a key-plate with a supplementary color plate. I mean two mutually complementary plates of equal importance. (As in music, a Bach fugue in two voices.) Here not colors, but tone values, play the chief role:

a. The tones are of equal value. For example, let us say the picture is composed of two shades, gray-blue and gray-red. A third shade will appear where the two overlap, gray-violet. We know from experience that it will be the darkest, and this must be taken into consideration in cutting the plates. So, with two blocks, three colors are produced. Since, in engraving, each block may have gradations within itself, even more tones will appear. [Illus. Nos. 25, 25A, 25B.]

b. The tones may be of unequal value; for example, black and brown. This immediately changes the style, and in order to avoid the impression of a key-plate, the darker tone must be given a subsidiary character, on which account it will be cut second. If the darker color takes up the formation of the picture only where the lighter leaves off, the essence of the style will be preserved. But no third color is produced. [Illus. Nos. 26, 26A, 26B.]

In both styles, one should get an impression of incompleteness in looking at a proof of each block alone. What one plate omits the other supplies, and there is no key-plate.

I assume that by now the difference is clear between building up a picture by one of the two methods described and by means of a key-plate with a subsidiary color plate. (As in music, one leading voice with subsidiary harmony.)

This, however, is not intended in any way as a pronouncement on artistic values, but only as a comprehensive view of the scope of a particular form of art. And I should like to repeat that nothing that I say about style and technique, and incidentally about art, need be taken as a standard by anyone else.

Whosoever thinks that he has mastered the art of sailing, and has steered his ship into hundreds of different ports under hundreds of varying conditions of wind and weather, knows that when he discusses these matters with another tried and true sailor, he will find that that man would have handled each of the experiences differently.

The feeling of anxiety with which an artist approaches each new woodcut will increase rather than diminish after a thousand blocks have been cut. The reverse would mean surrender to spiritual and technique routine, and I must confess that in moments of weariness or weakness I have longed for this. But a successful work of art is possible only with the mastery of the medium required at the moment.

It is easy to feel, but difficult to put into words, how much of a work of art springs from the imagination and how much from technical considerations. The use of the same technique ad infinitum I call routine. Routine sets in where further artistic development stops. I believe that this is the thing that all real artists dread the most.

from KIDNAPPED
by
Robert Louis Stevenson

from DON QUIXOTE

from the BOOKLOVER

from THE BOOKLOVER

from SAILOR'S ABC

from KIDNAPPED
by
Robert Louis Stevenson

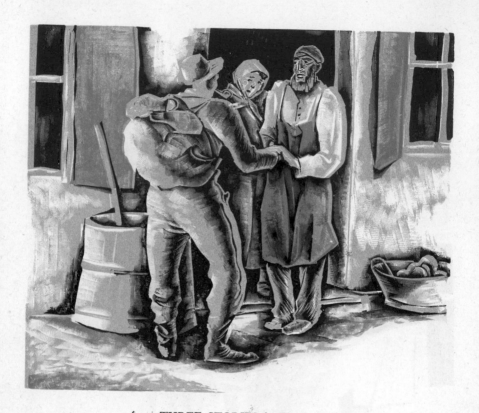

from THREE STORIES by Knute Hanson

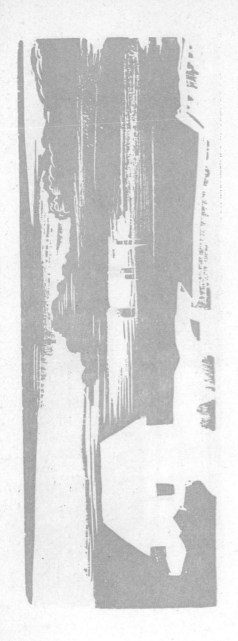
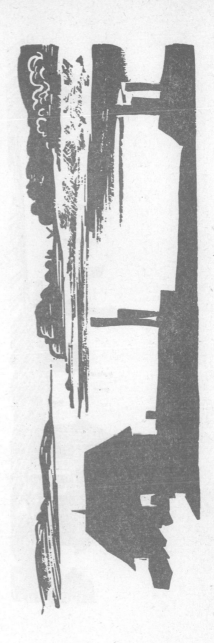

Design for Book Cover

The Woodcut in Book Illustration

CHAPTER VI

꘎ IN MY OPINION, it is in the use of the woodcut and the wood engraving that book illustration has attained its finest flowering.

A book illustrated with woodcuts can be one of the finest products of the printing press, if for no other reason than that the same principle, the relief process, applies to the printing of both type and illustrations. In this uniformity all good printers and publishers recognize an advantage over other methods of reproduction. It is of great importance from a technical and practical viewpoint that in most cases the illustrations and type can be printed at the same time.

Whether an illustration is printed from the original block or from a facsimile of it, the electrotype, is immaterial. A good electro reproduces the original to minute detail. And it is advisable to take good care of the original, since wood is not so hard as metal and in printing a large edition the block might be damaged or split. The making of an electro is cheaper than any method of reproducing an original drawing. On the other hand, the artist's fee for making his illustrations in woodcut is slightly higher, but that is justified on various grounds, and should not be an issue with the publisher in giving the commission.

It is to be regretted that, in general, woodcut illustration is comparatively little used. And one cannot claim any popularity for the woodcut illustration so long as only a few such books are found on the market.

Although the choice of literary material suitable for illustration is limited, there is still plenty of fertile ground left untilled by the illustrators. It is not easy to decide what literary material does lend itself for this purpose. But much as this subject tempts me, I must refrain from a discussion of it within the limits of this book.

But if an illustrated book is to be made, the text must be dominated by the illustrations, no matter how unobtrusively. For that reason I consider a book with only five full-page illustrations a most unsatisfactory production. At the five places in question the illustrations are too full, too conspicuous; the spaces in between appear empty; the interruptions are too great. In my opinion the illustrations should occupy from one-third to one-half of the printed space, and there should be no great gaps in their sequence.

Illustrations should appear in a book like residents of a house, not like Sunday visitors. They should not enter at certain high points of the story, but should accompany it all along the way. The illustrations may be very free, even digressing from the text, so long as they maintain the mood of the story, or they may follow in detail the events portrayed. This depends entirely upon the literary material and the style. In no case may they introduce a disturbing or foreign element. The ability to feel at one with his subject is one of the most important attributes of the illustrator.

There are some lovers of books who dislike illustrated books. As far as I have been able to analyze this dislike, it is based, in some instances, on books not really adapted to illustration; in others, on books whose text and pictures do not harmonize stylistically; or again, on books whose illustrations are merely a disturbing repetition of the events of the story.

From the point of view of aesthetics, an illustrated book may be considered a good job when pictures and text are interwoven like the threads of a fine English tweed, through whose grey background a single red or blue thread runs, distinct yet unobtrusive. Anyone who understands the beauty of type, the layout of the type page in relation to the white margins, the quality of paper, the placing of illustrations in the text, will turn the pages of such a book full of expectancy, especially if the book is richly illustrated and he can figure on being taken unawares every two or three pages by the varied placing of the pictures.

Perhaps it is because of my love for and obsession with the woodcut that I venture to express the opinion that no other original graphic medium is so suitable for book illustration. To produce proof of this I admit is not easy.

Probably the underlying reason is to be found in the handicraft, for both type and woodcut are made from blocks (metal or wood), with similar tools, and were made, perhaps, in earlier centuries, by one and the same hand.

Neither lithography nor etching is so well adapted as the woodcut to half- or quarter-page or even smaller illustrations within the text, for the process of printing from the lithographic stone or the etched copper plate does not have the same close relationship to the printing of type that the woodcut has. Consequently, it is a matter of the greatest nicety to make an etched or lithographic illustration an integral part of the printed page. To print it at the same time as the type is altogether impossible. The wood block, however, can be inserted without difficulty at any desired place in the text page. Also, there are difficulties in the selection of paper for intaglio and planographic printing. The range of papers suitable for the relief printing of woodcuts is much greater.

The various pros and cons so far given have been, for the most part, of a technical nature. Lithography and etching, it is true, could be used for full-page illustrations printed separately; but this again would introduce the full-page illustration, which I have already disposed of unqualifiedly.

Wherever purely artistic things evoke a response from the love of beauty in mankind, aesthetic sense, taste—whatever one may call it — the elements of style emerge as the arbiter and guide through the chaos and confusion of human emotions.

Style dictates proportion, direction, limitations. In considering the book as a whole, it prescribes choice of type, technique of the illustrations and their placing in relation to the text, whether black-and-white or colored, line or tonal, and their size in proportion to the paper and type page.

We may easily be reproached with drawing upon the term "emotion" when no more pertinent formula comes to hand. We artists, unfortunately, are compelled to use this word more often than we ourselves like. The more we rely on this "emotion" the more we experience its power, the more unequivocally it differentiates right and wrong, the less vague the concept is to us—and the more meaningless does it become when we speak of it before others.

So I see in the production of illustrations by lines or surfaces cut in relief the closest connection with printing type, which is likewise in relief. And this time I am speaking not from the point of view of technique, but of style. Not the combination of the lithographic stone and the greasy crayon, nor the etched lines of the copper plate, nor even the fine lines of the copper engraving can achieve the optical unity with the printed page that the lines and surfaces cut in wood possess.

With this I bow my head and patiently await the onslaught of my colleagues whose preference for etched illustrations, I must admit, is backed up with equal obstinacy. But I look forward to the attack without expectation of complete destruction. For if my own defense is not sufficient, I am assured of the support and protection of several unbiased experts outside of our artists' camp.

Illustration from DON QUIXOTE

If, in conclusion, I undertake to picture the genesis of an illustrated book, it is done only at the instigation of a particularly inspired and understanding booklover. This is in no way to be taken as an infallible recipe.

The best illustrated book will always be one whose literary content and style appeal especially to the illustrator—one that he has chosen himself, or one that he has written. In the latter case the whole proceeds naturally and smoothly, one thing growing out of another. Often the pictures predominate, the text playing a complementary, connecting role, both as to content and space. The development of such a book consists of a progressive shuttling back and forth between pictures and text. During the telling of the story there are pauses and the tale is carried forward by pictures, and vice versa. The illustrator holds all the strings and is his own director—what a grand feeling!

After the pages are made up, see where something must be added or omitted—where a chapter needs a tail-piece, perhaps. Then he can deliver to his publisher (if he has found one) a book complete in all respects.

The usual initiation of an illustrated book, however, is a commission from a publisher to supply pictures for a manuscript that he has on hand. I assume that the publisher has selected a story suitable for illustration and an artist suited to the job.

The illustrator begins to read in a mood of keen awareness and with closest attention. He is forced to curb his enjoyment of the story, absorbing its most intimate details with a certain coldbloodedness, of which, however, no trace must appear in the final pictures. The style of his illustrations will usually be determined after two or three pages, often after the very first sentence. It is an instinctive process and sets the character of the whole book at once. The book is practically complete in his mind; the hardest problem has been solved.

Practically, the style is established after several preliminary pen or brush sketches have been made, perhaps even a trial wood-cut. From this point on the artist can concentrate entirely upon the pictorial aspect of his illustrations. He has read the story pencil in hand, and has made notes in the text where, in his opinion, a picture was indicated.

Everyone in reading a story unconsciously builds up a mental image of the situation. The illustrator must retain these images with the greatest attention to detail, without at the same time making the mistake of giving a purely superficial reproduction of the chosen situations. A good illustration must show why the artist created it, must give something of the artist himself, be it only in what he emphasizes and what he leaves out as unimportant. It is not necessary to show the whole family at table every time they are mentioned in the story.

The style of speech, the period, the moods produced by descriptions or landscape, the spirit of the story—these elements form the mental background which determines a light or serious handling as well as the number and arrangement of the accompanying pictures.

Of how, in the last analysis, this is all achieved, I must of necessity keep silent. Once more, as we try to grasp these intangibles of artistic creation, they slip between our fingers.

But there still remains something to be said about the illustrated book as a whole and the book illustrated with woodcuts in particular. Cooperation between the illustrator and the printer is essential if the book is to be a beautiful typographic production. If the illustrator himself knows type, composition, paper, press-work and binding, so much the better. Good illustrations alone do not make a good book, if they are made without consideration for the printed page as a whole; and a good piece of composition may not, by a long shot, fit in with the pictures. Mutual appropriateness, therefore, is the requisite which determines which should be planned first, the illustrations or the text page. A satisfactory result will aways be obtained when the designer is given a free hand in all respects. He will be only too willing to accept the suggestions of compositors and pressmen and take advantage of their specialized knowledge.

The best assurance for the creation of a "fine" book lies in the way in which the publisher gives the commission. An intelligent publisher is well aware of the parts played by all the factors involved. For his part, he has done all he could for the success of a publication when he has chosen his artist and his printer. All that remains for him to do is to set the amount of the honorarium and the date of publication. Any further interference is only harmful to himself. The artist and the printer will feel themselves under such obligation to his generosity and restraint, not to mention the joy of the work for its own sake, that they cannot choose but give their best.

An illustrated book is doomed to be born crippled the moment a publisher lets fall any remarks likely to cramp the artist's freedom. To enlarge upon this subject would be highly amusing, but would require a chapter to itself. My own adventures as a beginner, and the experiences of my advanced pupils which I lived through vicariously as their teacher, have been both cramping and dishcartening and always humiliating.

*   *   *

If a book is to be illustrated with woodcuts, it is very helpful to the wood engraver to have the text set up in galleys before him as he works. He can then occasionally paste up a proof of a woodcut with the text in actual page size and study the effect. In this way he can decide whether a picture should be placed at the beginning of a chapter, in the middle or the end, and on a right- or left-hand page. This also permits him to regulate the size of his cuts depending upon the amount of text in a chapter. During the period of making the illustrations he works under a prolonged. self-enforced tension and inspiration.

So, page by page, he fashions the whole book. It is obvious that the woodcut is particularly adapted to this kind of interweaving of picture and text. One cannot deal so easily with an original drawing, aside from the fact that usually it is drawn larger than it is to appear in the book. The lithographic and etching techniques are not so flexible, for they require much more complicated equipment.

All the tools for woodcutting can be stuck in your pocket if necessary. I have them with me on every trip, whether in a remote inn in the mountains or in the cabin of my sailboat.

ACKNOWLEDGMENT

Grateful acknowledgment is made to the publishers who have granted permission to reproduce in this volume works by Hans Alexander Mueller which first appeared in their publications.

"Don Quixote" published by Random House, New York City; "Son of the Danube" by Boris Petroff, published by the Viking Press, New York City; "Dr. Jekyll and Mr. Hyde" by R. L. Stevenson, published by Peter Pauper Press, Mt. Vernon, New York; "A Conrad Argosy" published by Doubleday, Doran, New York City; the wood engravings of Abraham Lincoln and Thomas Jefferson in Funk & Wagnalls New Standard Encyclopaedia, published by Unicorn Press, Brooklyn, N. Y.; the wood engraving of Thomas Masaryk in "The Living Thoughts Library," published by Longmans, Green & Company, New York City.